THE GREAT AMERICANS SERIES

Harriet Tubman

By Kathie Billingslea Smith

Illustrated by James Seward

Cover Portrait: Joseph Forte

Julian Messner
New York

Copyright © 1988 by Ottenheimer Publishers, Inc. All rights reserved including the right of reproduction in whole or in part in any form. Published by Julian Messner, a division of Silver Burdett Press, Inc., Simon & Schuster, Inc., Prentice Hall Bldg., Englewood Cliffs, NJ 07632. JULIAN MESSNER and colophon are trademarks of Simon & Schuster, Inc. PRINTED IN MEXICO. 10 9   8   7   6   5   4   3   2   1

Library of Congress Cataloging-in-Publication Data

Smith, Kathie Billingslea.
   Harriet Tubman / by Kathie Billingslea Smith ; illustrated by
James Seward.
      p.   cm. — (The Great Americans series)
   ISBN 0-671-67513-3 (lib. bdg.) : $7.79
   1. Tubman, Harriet, 1820?-1913—Juvenile literature. 2. Slaves—
United States—Biography—Juvenile literature. 3. Afro-Americans—
Biography—Juvenile literature. 4. Underground railroad—Juvenile
literature. I. Seward, James E. II. Title. III. Series.
E444.T82S63   1988
305.5′67′0924—dc19
   [B]   88-13612
                                     CIP
                                     AC

In the early 1800's, a man named Edward Brodas owned a large plantation in Dorchester County on the eastern shore of Maryland. He also owned many slaves. They worked hard all day, without pay, in his stables, cookhouse, orchards and fields. Mr. Brodas lived in what was called "The Big House"—a fine brick mansion with lovely furniture. His slaves lived in windowless one-room log cabins. They slept on piles of blankets and kept warm by huddling near the fireplace on winter nights.

It was in a shack like this, in the year 1820, that a baby girl was born to Harriet Greene and her husband, Benjamin Ross. They called their daughter Araminta and nicknamed her Minta.

"We will call her 'Harriet' when she is older," they decided.

◄ Slaves gathering wood.

As a young child, Minta played with her ten brothers and sisters and other slave children under the watchful eye of a slave woman who was too old to work. Minta's mother worked in The Big House. She hoped that Minta would be trained to work there, too, as a cook or a nurse. But Minta loved the outdoors and was happiest when she was outside.

At the age of six, Minta was hired out to work for a neighbor who was a weaver. Minta hated working inside and missed her family terribly. She became quite sick with measles and bronchitis and was sent back to the Brodas plantation. Her mother nursed her back to health, but for the rest of her life, Minta spoke in a deep, husky voice.

Two more times Minta was hired out to work for others. She was often treated cruelly. Her back became laced with scars from many whippings. Many years later she said, "...there were good masters and mistresses, as I've heard tell, but I didn't happen to come across any of them."

When Minta was ten, she was sent to work in a neighbor's fields. She worked from dawn to dusk loading wood on wagons, splitting rails, and plowing crops. Although the work was hard, Minta was happy to be outdoors.

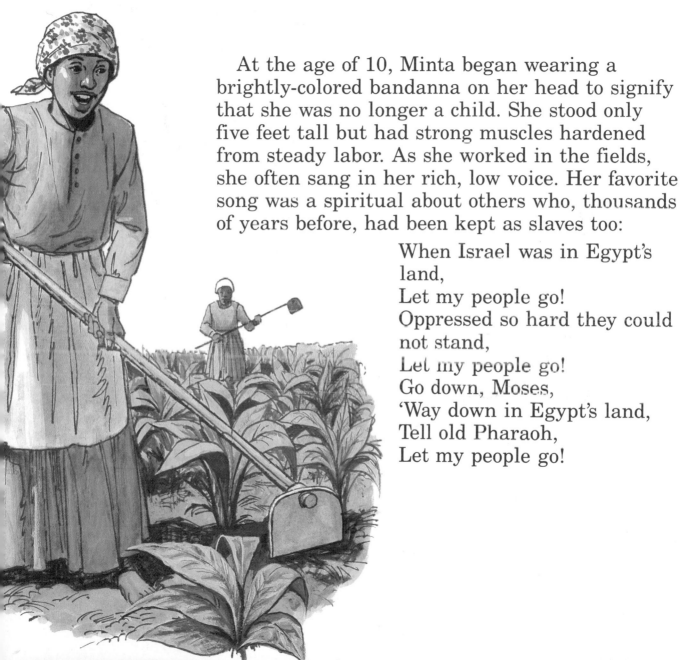

At the age of 10, Minta began wearing a brightly-colored bandanna on her head to signify that she was no longer a child. She stood only five feet tall but had strong muscles hardened from steady labor. As she worked in the fields, she often sang in her rich, low voice. Her favorite song was a spiritual about others who, thousands of years before, had been kept as slaves too:

When Israel was in Egypt's land,
Let my people go!
Oppressed so hard they could not stand,
Let my people go!
Go down, Moses,
'Way down in Egypt's land,
Tell old Pharaoh,
Let my people go!

In America at this time, slavery was legal in Maryland and many other southern states. In nearby Pennsylvania and farther north, slavery was not allowed.

Life was cruelly hard for many slaves. Because of recent slave uprisings, white owners took away what little freedom the slaves had. Strict laws said that slaves could not walk alone on a road without a pass. Slaves were not allowed to learn to read or write. They could not even hold their own church meetings.

Minta and the other slaves hated the life they were forced to lead. They often thought of freedom and knew that if they could get to the North, they could be free.

They heard stories about slaves who escaped north to freedom. The runaways seemed to disappear from sight as if they had gone on an underground road. Minta and the other slaves heard there were friendly people—black and white—who sheltered runaways and helped them travel north. Soon everyone began talking about an underground railroad—a network of people who secretly led slaves to freedom. The idea thrilled Minta.

◄ Some slaves learned to read without the knowledge of their owners.

But white men patrolled the countryside on horseback, looking for runaways. If caught, the slaves were brought back in chains and punished severely. Some slaves were branded with an "R." Others had the front part of a foot cut off. Some slaves were whipped and even killed.

Minta still dreamed of being free. Late at night, she liked to lie down in the grass and gaze up at the sky. She noticed that the stars changed their positions each night. Only one bright star stayed still.

"That's the North Star," her father, Ben, told her. "Look, the stars of the Big Dipper point right at it."

"It looks like a special star—so shiny and bright," said Minta.

"It's the best star there is," Ben replied. "The North Star points the way to freedom."

In the fall of 1830, Mr. Brodas held a cornhusking bee. Minta and other slaves from all around came to help shuck the harvested corn.

As night fell, a slave slipped away in the darkness. Before he got very far, he was caught by the overseer.

"Help me tie up this runaway!" the overseer ordered Minta.

She refused to help. The slave broke away and escaped again. Angrily, the overseer threw a heavy weight at him. He missed,

and the weight hit Minta on the forehead. She was knocked unconscious, bleeding from a huge gash.

For months she lay in bed without moving. The next spring she recovered, but for the rest of her life she suffered from horrible headaches. Sometimes she would unexpectedly fall into deep sleeps from which she could not be awakened for hours. Harriet, as everyone now called her, wore the large scar on her head like a badge of courage.

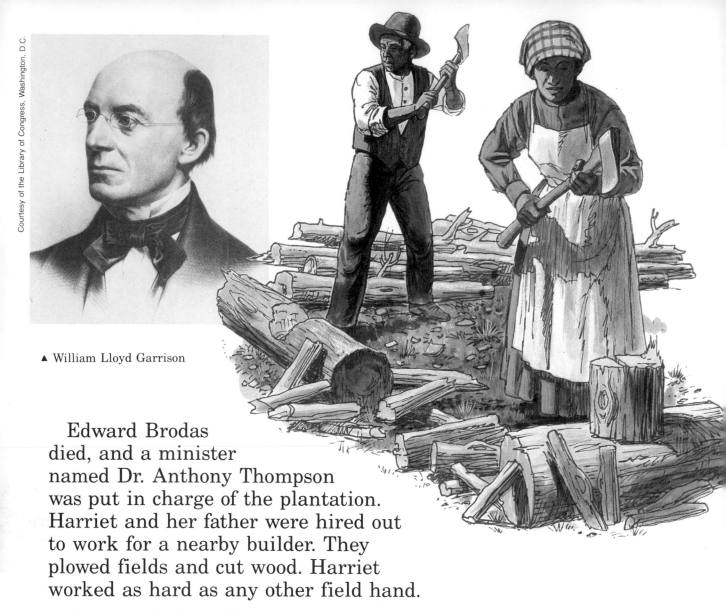

▲ William Lloyd Garrison

Edward Brodas
died, and a minister
named Dr. Anthony Thompson
was put in charge of the plantation.
Harriet and her father were hired out
to work for a nearby builder. They
plowed fields and cut wood. Harriet
worked as hard as any other field hand.

Ben taught her all that he knew about animals. He showed
her which plants were good to eat and which ones could be used
for medicine. Harriet learned how to walk through the woods
without making a sound.

"You walk like an Indian," her father told her.

Harriet was pleased to hear his praise. Deep in her heart she knew that she would use her new skills someday.

In the North, people began to speak out against slavery. William Lloyd Garrison published an anti-slavery newspaper called *The Liberator*.

Harriet fell in love with a free black man named John Tubman. They were married in 1844 and lived in a small cabin by themselves. Slaves were not forbidden to marry free blacks. But the slaves were still owned by the masters after any marriages. Years went by. Harriet never stopped dreaming about being free. Over and over in her head she planned how she would escape north to freedom. John Tubman laughed at her.

"I am happy here," he said. "I won't go with you."

Harriet felt very sad. She knew that he wouldn't help her.

In the fall of 1849, Harriet learned that she and her brothers were to be sold to a Georgia trader.

People began to speak out against slavery. ▶

At dusk Harriet gathered some food and tied it up in an old bandanna. Then she crept through the woods to a nearby house. The white woman who lived there had promised Harriet help if she ever needed it. True to her word, she gave Harriet the directions to the houses of other people who would help her as she traveled north to freedom.

Harriet was afraid that she might suddenly fall asleep, as she often did, and be caught. With a prayer in her heart, she began her journey on the Underground Railroad. For weeks she slept by day and traveled by night. She walked until her feet bled. She hid in haystacks, barns, and attics.

Free black families, white Quaker families, friendly German farmers, and many others risked their own safety to give Harriet food and shelter on her journey.

Each night, Harriet looked to the North Star for direction. After traveling nearly ninety miles, she finally reached freedom in Pennsylvania. She crossed the state line at dawn.

"I looked at my hands to see if I was the same person now I was free," she said. "There was such a glory over everything, the sun came like gold through the trees, and over the fields, and I felt like I was in heaven."

Courtesy of the Library of Congress, Washington, D.C.

▲ Some runaway slaves were caught and returned to their owners.

Harriet traveled on to Philadelphia. However, she was lonesome and missed her family.

"There was no one to welcome me to the land of freedom," she said later. "I was a stranger in a strange land."

But Harriet loved her new-found freedom. She could go anywhere in the North without a pass. She could work at any job she liked, and the money she earned was hers to use as she pleased. Harriet vowed then and there to help other slaves escape to freedom and to welcome them to a new home in the North.

For a year Harriet worked as a cook in a hotel in Philadelphia. She saved most of the money she earned.

In December 1850, one of Harriet's sisters and her family escaped from the plantation on Maryland's eastern shore and sailed, at night, to Baltimore. Harriet traveled south to meet them and guided them safely to Philadelphia.

The next spring, Harriet traveled back to the Brodas plantation and brought away one of her brothers and two other men. That fall she again risked her life and went back to get her husband John Tubman. She was crushed to find that he had a new wife and did not want to go with her. Instead she helped another small group of slaves escape north.

Each of these journeys took weeks. Harriet led the slaves, traveling by night through forests. She often dressed like a man to disguise herself and move more easily through the woods. Her courage never wavered.

"I just hold steady onto the Lord," she often said. "He will take care of me."

Soon it was no longer safe for slaves to stay in Philadelphia or other cities in the North. The Fugitive Slave Law required the people of the North to return to the South any runaway slaves they found. This did not frighten Harriet.

"After that," she said, "I wouldn't trust Uncle Sam with my people no longer, but I brought them all clear off to Canada."

For six years, Harriet spent winters working in Canada and summers working in Philadelphia or Cape May, New Jersey. She bought a small house in Auburn, New York. Each spring and each fall, she traveled back into slave territory to bring more slaves to freedom.

Harriet became a legend in the slave cabins along the eastern shore of Maryland. The slaves called her "Moses" because, like the Moses of long ago, she led her people out of slavery.

When Harriet arrived at the plantations, she crept quietly to the slaves' doors and softly sang "Go Down Moses" in her deep, rich voice.

"Moses is here! Moses is here!" The message was whispered up and down the rows of slave cabins.

Those who wanted to run away north gathered food and waited for another signal. On the next clear night, when the North Star shone brightly, Harriet signalled to them from the woods by imitating a whippoorwill's call or a hoot owl's hoot. Then they began their long journey together. Sometimes Harriet fell into deep sleeps that lasted for minutes or hours. But she always woke up safely to continue on her journey to freedom.

By 1858, Harriet had guided more than 300 slaves to safety in the North!

The slave-holders on the Eastern Shore offered a reward of $40,000.00 for her capture.

During her time spent in the North, Harriet fearlessly traveled from city to city and spoke before large crowds. In her rich, expressive voice, she told of her struggles to guide other slaves to freedom.

The United States was a country split over the issue of slavery. In November 1860, Abraham Lincoln was elected President of the

◄ President Abraham Lincoln

United States. Soon after that, many southern states left the Union to form the Confederate States of America. On April 14, 1861, the Confederate Army captured Fort Sumter in South Carolina. This was the beginning of the Civil War—a battle that pitted the North against the South. Americans fought against Americans.

◄ President Lincoln signing the Emancipation Proclamation.

The war thrust Harriet into a new role. The Governor of Massachusetts asked her to help her people in a different way. Harriet traveled by boat to Port Royal, an island off of South Carolina. The Confederate fort there had been captured by the Union Army and was filled with slaves who had run away from their owners, hoping to find safety. Many of the slaves were starving, ill, or hurt. Some had traveled hundreds of miles to reach safety. Harriet worked as a nurse there, helping the slaves to regain their health. She used her knowledge of herbs to brew medicines that saved many lives.

In January of 1863, President Lincoln signed the Emancipation Proclamation. It

stated that all slaves
in the Confederate
states were free. But
many southern slave owners refused to let their slaves go.

With a musket in her hand and a canteen by her side, Harriet sailed with Union soldiers on gunboats up the rivers and marshes of the South Carolina low country. She gathered up slaves working in the rice fields and filled boat after boat with them. The slaves were afraid of the Union soldiers and would never have gone with them except for the friendly, reassuring presence of Harriet Tubman. On one trip, nearly 800 slaves were rescued. One Union general called Harriet "a most remarkable woman, and invaluable as a scout."

In 1864, Harriet returned to her home in Auburn, New York, to nurse her elderly parents and help wounded soldiers in a nearby hospital.

The Civil War ended on April 9, 1865, with the surrender of the Confederate forces. A week later, President Lincoln was shot and killed. In December of that year, the Thirteenth Amendment to the Constitution was ratified, ending slavery forever.

After the war, Harriet's house became known as a haven for the homeless. Anyone who needed food or shelter was welcome there. At any given time, three to ten people lived with her.

◄ Elizabeth Cady Stanton

Susan B. Anthony ▲

Harriet cleaned houses and peddled vegetables from door-to-door to earn money to feed them. She was never given any pay or pension for the years she served with the Union Army.

In March of 1869, Harriet married a man named Nelson Davis. They had many happy years together, but he was ill with tuberculosis and died in 1888.

Harriet became active in the fight for women's rights and spoke at rallies with Elizabeth Cady Stanton and Susan B. Anthony.

In 1903, she gave her house and twenty-five acres of land that she had purchased to the African Methodist Episcopal Zion Church in Auburn to be used for a home for the sick and homeless. She lived there until her death on March 10, 1913, at the age of ninety-three.

Harriet was given a military funeral. A year later, thousands of people from all over the United States gathered in Auburn to dedicate a memorial in her honor. Today Harriet's home on South Street in Auburn is kept in her memory by the A.M.E. Zion Church.

Harriet Tubman was a remarkable woman. She spent her life helping others. She held firm in the belief that freedom was a right all people should enjoy. Harriet worked as a field hand, a nurse, a speaker, and a scout. But she is best remembered for her work as a conductor on the Underground Railroad, leading hundreds of people from slavery to freedom.

"On my Underground Railroad," Harriet said with pride, "I never ran my train off the track, and I never lost a passenger."